VERSES FROM MY NIB

Sushmita Nanda

QUICK READS

by Writersgram Publications

VERSES FROM MY NIB
Fiction by Sushmita Nanda

First Impression: February 2020

© Sushmita Nanda

ISBN: 978-9389244588

Published by: Writersgram Publications, New Delhi

www.writersgram.com
publications@writersgram.com

Maximum Retail Price: ₹ 180/-

Sushmita Nanda asserts the moral right to be identified as the author of this book.

HOW CAN I?

How can I forget the desolate road?
That walk an extra mile with me,
When you flee.
How can I forget those tears?
That let my emotions flow,
When I feel low.
How can I forget my diary?
That act as a canvas,
When I am anxious.
How can I forget my pen?
That help my words bleed,
Whenever in need.
How can I forget my pillow?
That soak the salty water,
Which fall each time your name I utter.
How can I forget that rose?
That still prevail in copies,
Holding back memories.
How can I forget my books?
That never complaint or demand,
When I reprimand.
How can I forget my best friend?
Who is my armour throughout,
Either I'm sure or in doubt.
How can I forget?
How can I?

HAPPINESS

Come and find me,
In the melodies of your favourite song,
Come and find me,
In the caress that gives you warmth,
Come and find me,
In the book you can relate,
Come and find me,
In the blessing of grandparents,
Come and find me,
In the selfless deed you've done,
Come and find me,
In the lunch box mum packs each day,
Come and find me,
But wait,
What are you seeking?
Who am I?
Come and find,
"HAPPINESS."

SELF LOVE

I ride the horses of my thought,
They lead me to an empty sought,
I wander like a cloud,
Unaware of what I seek in crowd,
Maybe someone who can help pick my pieces,
And fix them with backstiches,
Then I see a handsome lad,
Glancing his smile I feel glad,
Oh my my! If he's the one,
My heart winked on my next action,
I move ahead giving him no damn,
'Self Love ' first said dad's telegram,
Recalling those words I return home,
Gathering my ashes I sleep alone.

FRIGHT OF BEING JUDGED

He sits alone in the corner,
Searching something he doesn't know,
Just tapping on his mobile phone,
Switching from social sites to game,
Is he a geek?
No, not at all,
He is just like you and me,
But a little afraid of being judged,
By the people and the crowd,
He needed to be understood,
And being told that -
You are no sinner if you are jobless,
You are not a burden if you are 22,
Still are dependent on your family,
Focus a little more on your aim,
None can stop you to hit the goal.

TONIGHT I SHALL WRITE

Tonight, I shall write,
The most agonist verse,
A saga of a maiden,
And her adventures;
She sings her grieves,
Dances her sorrow,
Still manages to believe,
For a better tomorrow;
Confesses to herself, every night
To be bold and face the plight,
Not bright she might be as sunlight,
But surely her smile can bring anyone delight.

NOSTALGIA

Saw you smiling through my window,
My eyes went teary in a moment or so,
Haven't seen you in long run,
With you it had always been fun,
Glad you're doing great,
Wish you could ever relate,
To the torment I endured,
Leaving me on the path that you ensured,
Yea! Circumstances were much easier to blame,
For you were too less into the game.

DEVILS IN DISGUISE

When you will grow plump and stout,
They have eyes on you without any doubt,
Like a ripen mango or an orange,
You will be looked as something strange,
Those breasts, one day when become loud,
To grab them, then be the desire of every man in the crowd,
Oh! The more the curves,
The more pleasure she deserves,
Moment you hold a notion,
Welcomed you will be in the world of feminism,
Damn! She has got big butts,
Look she dresses like sluts,
Girl, asking for the salary same,
Has lost her mind and got insane,
Modern women are easy to catch,
For it is easier with them to play detach.

BLOT IS JUST A MYTH

Listen and obey,
To what they have to say,
Oh girl! Follow,
You can otherwise cause dismay.
Pretty face,
Of a lower race,
You are nothing,
But a blot on grace.
Dear society,
You bring me disability,
Suppressing my folk is an act of pity,
Nurture me,
I am an asset not any liability,
You compel me to abide by the norms,
Which are made by some orthodox worms,
Making me slave of your terms,
Each night evoke in me thousand storms.

SOMEDAY

You can never understand,
The way I feel when I'm unnoticed ,
Where I could have been noticed,
You can never understand,
The silent scream which I make,
When I am treated secondary,
You can never understand,
The hundred thousand emotions,
Which rage in me when I'm said mercy on,
You can never understand,
The grief which is held within,
Since I have been treated as an object,
You can never understand,
The multiple thoughts that come to my mind,
And make me contemplate myself,
You can never understand,
But I wish someday you could!

WISDOM TO WISE

13

Not all those who cry are weak,

Not all those who keep quiet are geek,

Not all those who know language can speak,

To cry your heart out needs courage,

To remain quiet and respect doesn't make you average,

To know where to speak is great knowledge.

WOMEN

She maybe a wife, or a daughter,
A teacher or a mother,
But above all she is always a mentor,
Being literate or not ,
Can never question her slot,
She is as important as a dot,
In a sentence,
She knows no fence,
Her life, perhaps mess,
Still she wears smile with confidence,
No special day can celebrate her virtues,
For greater she is ,
And our thanks will always be few.

AN ODE TO MY MUSE

I sing this hymn to all those eternal muses,
Who bring me the strength to rectify the fuses,
I sit back and contemplate what would I be,
If I were not distinct,
Feeling a little more than normal,
Having a transcendental vision,
Blessed with all these skills,
Still there is something that kills,
A fear-
A threat-
They may criticise me,
For having creating an explicit fable,
To moral grounds which attach no cable,
Being an ardent scribe,
I jot down every bribe,
Caused me to frame a peculiar piece,
And providing me an unusual ease,
I bled with the mighty sword,
So that all those readers can taste each word,
That language might seem obscene,
Truly that is what we speak in routine,
I rely on myself for what I say,
Merely I write to make someone gay,
Not like Shakespeare and Pope,
I am renowned,
Nevertheless I write with a hope,
That my perspective may take you to a ground.

THE CHANGE

I am the breeze,
Untouched and liberated,
From all your tantrums;
I am the sky,
Too high to reach,
But setting the limit;
I am the question,
Unanswered-
Free from vague replies;
I am the river,
Which paves it's own way,
Through hills and valleys;
I am the way I am,
I am THE CHANGE.

BEAUTY – AN ILLUSION

Beauty is in the eyes of beholder, really?
Beauty is in the heart that feels okay even if it's not the
same,
Beauty is in the help that you do ,
Beauty is accepting them with flaws,
Beauty is understanding and supporting no matter if you
are the most broken,
Never stop sharing,
This world would be beautiful.

THE WOLF

I am a loner- THE WOLF,
With you I have not attached any hook,
I hunt solely in the dark,
Passing through the fields in my stark,
I am at rise on the full moon,
That spark to me is a boon,
The predator I am, so dangerous,
For your health I could be heinous,
You cannot get away my gaze,
The skill of mine may set you amaze,
Night allures me like anything,
Whereas light to me seems nothing,
I rule the black,
For that's the best time to attack,
That flesh of yours is a bait,
To chew that soft skin I cannot wait.

INTROSPECTION

Introspect and tell,
Are you a man?
Speak out loud,
If your worth being called a human?
Think again,
What did you do inhumane?
You de-flowered her,
And you wish your wife to be a chaste woman,
Do you stand somewhere on those parameters?
Do you count yourself as noble ?
Having being slept with many,
You can't accept your bride to be any,
Your aspirations are huge,
But mind it, you're a scrooge,
Questioning her character,
Leaves you as an abuser,
You might consider yourself,
As a greater product of Aryan,
Oh dear! Your deeds are worst,
Than that of Satan,
The moment you'd be reduced to ashes,
For once recall all the bruises,
Recollect all the crimes,
Now wonder all those sins were not mere but prime.

SELF DOUBT

My soul screams and my mind shouts,
"You damned human are full of doubts,"
My touch is that of Midas,
One day I'll have to alas!
For the loss which I am to face,
Seems I am unsuited for this race,
This salty water burns my cheek,
As I let it flow with emotions weak,
My lips begin to tremble,
Words I utter fumble,
I am imprisoned in my vices,
My virtues insipid lacking spices,
I smile to ears having a belief,
It's okay not to be okay is a relief,
Till date my tears soak in pillows,
Revealing no scar though hit by arrows,
Apparently you may name me a Masochist,
To me I am a realist,
I am aware of my eccentric behaviour,
To my rescue I myself have to be the savoir,
I culminate here with a token of gratitude,
And apologies if my words sound crude.

NIGHTMARE

Again I wake up to a nightmare,
To snatch everything from me someone dared,
It seems a great blunder,
Leaving me in thunder,
Quivering and shivering out of fear,
Don't know any escape near,
Unlike ever, the path is desolate,
I walk there without any mate,
Seeking my serenity,
I pass the woods of chaos;
There's no tranquillity,
Just unfathomable moss;
My eyes opened to a sudden break,
And saved me from believing in something fake.

OH HUMAN!

Oh human! Oh human!
We all are God's creation,
In the race of meeting expectation,
We have already achieved our destination,
But don't know how to give it recognition,
Which takes away satisfaction,
Leaving permanent accommodation,
We seek occupation,
Still we don't find affection,
And get disheartened,
In God's devotion,
We attain emancipation,
And live rest of the life,
In this blissful sensation,
Recalling the irony of life,
That oh human! Oh human!
We all are God's creation.

NOT YOUR GIRL

I am not a girl,
Who goes to party and wanders with friends,
I am not a girl,
Who puts up makeup to glam up,
I am not a girl,
Who dresses western to look pretty,
I am not a girl,
Who wishes of expensive jewellery,
Rather,
I am a girl,
Who loves the smell of books,
I am a girl,
Who adores Augustus Waters,
I am a girl,
Who stays up late just to make two lovers meet,
I am a girl,
Who fantasises of surrounded by nature,
I may not be your type for I am a different creature.

GRATITUDE

Blessings are hailing,
From here there and everywhere,
Never knew you were the roof,
Saving me from the good,
Glad you taught me to be in dark,
For now I'm enjoying every spark,
I used to weep in the rain,
Today I enjoy dews on grain,
I've had enough of sadness,
It's time to embrace little happiness.

TOUCH-ME-NOT

I am just a part of nature,
A little creature,
I feel tickle with every touch,
I giggle and maybe react too much,
With that sensation I collapse,
The baby enjoys and claps,
Playing for hours,
He looked at the stars,
The moon tonight shone a little bright,
Baby's face glisten in that light,
I hold my gaze,
With his laugh the sky ablaze,
I'm THE TOUCH-ME-NOT,
The plant you'll be playful with at any spot.

THE EMPIRE

My home has been snatched,
When my mate detached,
Flowers stop to bloom,
I begin to move towards doom,
Clouds start to cry,
Happiness seem to fly,
Darkness all around,
No merry in surround,
As the snow melt,
Nothing left to be felt.
That's when,
I dry my tears,
I fight all fears,
I stand tall,
Not trying to fall,
I wear my heels,
Ecstatic it feels,
I build the castle,
With no tussle,
I write my story,
Using words of glory.

FOCUS ON WHAT YOU WANT

Locked up in a room,

Waiting for my doom,

I'm neither sinner nor a saint,

Just wish my sadness to faint,

Sabotaged by my own people,

I appreciate my heart's still not feeble.

For now, I yearn to cry,

Tears deny coming out don't know why,

Somewhere amidst the crowd,

I shout out loud,

My words on mute,

For the people so brute,

They barely care about what I to say,

So busy in their works they've got no heed to pay.

Learnt a lesson,

Follow your passion,

Do great in it,

In your shoes society will try to fit,

Then it's your turn to show them,

That you're no less than a growing stem.

Rock your own world,

Happiness will eventually be swirled.

I'M SPECIAL- NOT REALLY

Why do you have to be so stiff,
I feel like jumping off the cliff,
You need to understand the stuff,
Meeting people and exchanging hugs is as trivial as a
cigarette puff,
Maybe I'm too open and you too rigid,
Our love is getting frigid,
I bleed rose,
Need to justify my pose,
Oh damn! Keep calm,
Seems my hand is unfit for your Palm,
Still I wake up this Morning,
With my heart groaning,
Asking my heart to shut up,
A smile, to start my day I manage to develop,
Inside it shout out loud,
For pleasing others your opinion is not needed to
enshroud,
Happiness is a far cry,
I'm unfit no matter how much I try,
Whatever I do goes wrong,
"I'm sorry, so sorry" keep singing this song.

MEN

Yes, they cry,
Yes, they're emotional,
Yes, they respect women,
Yes, they're not dominant,
Yes, they feel,
Yes, they're kind,
Yes, they like pink colour,
Yes, they love being pampered,
Yes, they're "MEN."

HUMANITY

I sigh! I sigh!
Humanity is the farthest cry.
I wonder why,
After witnessing something wrong we turn a blind eye?
Pity, I'm not the person you can rely.
I sigh! I sigh!
Humanity is the farthest cry.
If lowering you makes me high,
Who give me the right to make you cry?
When your tears I cannot dry.
I ponder again,
What is more inhumane,
The raping of women,
Or trafficking of human?
A blot on humanity,
The bias in name of community,
Terrorism and it's cruelty.
I pity! I sigh!
We are killing innocence,
In the so called society that is hi-Fi.
And yet ,
A stranger helps me cross the road,
An unknown call to share the load,
That feeling of home in abroad,
Restores my faith,
Restores my Grace,
In the milk of human kindness.

It is alive -
It is not dead -
Not as yet.
I sigh! I sigh! Humanity is not the farthest cry.

AM I?

Am I less woman,
If I wear my confidence?
Am I less man,
If I respect women?
Am I less human,
If I love animals equally?
Am I less sacred,
If I bleed a week in the month?
Am I less social,
If I have more real friends?
Am I less respectful,
If I speak my mind out?
Am I less than you,
If I let you stand by my side?
Am I less?
Am I?

MOTHERHOOD

They whisper,
They murmur,
In groups of three or four,
They simply chatter.
Think once,
Give her another chance,
And an empathetic glance.
She's not sterile,
Neither futile.
She can give birth,
She can also be a mother,
Don't gossip like that further.
When they talk shit,
When say she doesn't fit,
Humanity they omit.
They whisper,
They murmur,
In groups of three or four,
They simply chatter.
After so many years of misconceive,
She finally achieve.
A baby in her womb,
A bud ready to bloom,
That sets her free from doom.
She become mom,
She delivered a daughter instead of son,
She again become a part of fun,

But she's strong so she did not shun.
This time she already knew,
They will forget after talking for days a few.
Because it's their habit,
They whisper,
They murmur,
In groups of three or four,
They simply chatter.

STAND TALL

You let all the seasons test you,
Be it scorching heat of summer,
Or stormy wind of Autumn,
You stand strong enjoying the snowfall in winter,
And you blossom spreading your aroma,
In the springs of April,
Like you have been kept protected
Of all the hindrances,
You flow at ease with gentle breeze,
Invincible and inevitable.

FORGIVE ME

I'm not a toy,
I'm not a public pleaser,
I'm not a peace maker,
But I'm a human,
I do make mistakes,
I do let you down,
I do fail to meet the expectations,
Does all my flaws make you leave me?
Does my wail really look fake to you?
Does that mean I'm no more yours?
Pardon me for my wrongs,
Pardon me to be a part of your life,
Pardon me to trouble you,
No more I'll be around you,
No more I'll embarrass you,
No more I'll be there,
Bid me farewell,
For its the last time,
I'm knocking at your door.

MARITAL RAPE

Liberty, oh Yea!
Breathing air of freedom,
For my body made of clay,
But not a toy in your dome.
You're my fiance,
Not allowed to do barbarism.
I cried aloud 'No',
You forced chauvinism,
Made it like I bestow,
To you it's a custom,
Mandatory to follow.
Now the love only prevails in our marriage album,
As independence is something I've forgotten months ago,
Another attempt of euphemism,
I suffer everyday.
'Happy first marriage anniversary' smirked humanism,
Marital rape is a mere term people say.

FOR THE FIRST TIME

Alas! That woeful evening,
I remember everything,
Those unheard screams,
Those shattered dreams,
I was merrily enjoying my teenage,
When they shove me in the baggage,
The night was dark and cold,
A girl for pieces of paper was sold.
I refused To be touched,
They smirked,
For I was in their clutch.
This was the first time,
I had been touched differently,
I bled on the sheet,
I wailed silently.
That scary night I was transformed,
Transformed from to a kid to woman,
I got no chance to be a girl,
I pity on me and thee,
You didn't let me what I wished to be.
I'm sad for myself and every other girl
Who undergoes the same,
We're not the ones to tame.
Revival of memories,
From that horrific night,
Sends chill through the spine,
Alas! That woeful evening, I remember everything.

PERHAPS

Perhaps we lay under the same stars,
Perhaps our hearts beat on same rhythms,
Perhaps we share the same soul,
Perhaps our desires are same,
Perhaps we hold together,
Perhaps our destinations are different,
Perhaps we sail on the same boat,
Perhaps our sailors are distinct,
Perhaps we have seen the same dream,
Perhaps our paths are diverse,
Perhaps we are bonded with a chord so strong,
Perhaps our distinct ways bring us together,
Perhaps we are apart,
Perhaps our hearts are broken,
But one day we will meet,
And mend our broken hearts,
Attain the dreams seen together,
Explore the world on the same boat,
That will be the day,
Perhaps will not exist,
And surety will replace it.

PATRIARCHY

O men! You let me not rise,
You subdue my worth,
You doubt my efforts,
You make me inferior,
Dear patriarchy,
I know it's difficult,
For you to allow me liberty,
But believe me, I am no kid,
In need of your security,
I am a grown up,
An independent woman,
I am self sufficient,
Let me! Let me!! Let me!!!
SUSTAIN,
Try me once,
I am no disdain;
You shatter my confidence,
With the words of filth,
Still I stand tall,
Besides being blamed,
My journey is no easy- as believed by all,
I will adhere to my notion,
And turn in reality the things I claimed;
O men! Even if you not let me rise,
I will fly to your surprise.

VEILS AND MASKS

Veils over veils,
Masks over masks,
Just another face,
With every question you ask;
A pain, a grief, a torment,
It's all kept safe,
Behind a smile so taint.
Veils over veils,
Masks over masks,
Just another face,
With every question you ask;
There's envy and distrust,
Betrayal and relations rust,
Fake compassions can entrust,
Forming foundations of dust.
Veils over veils,
Masks over masks,
Just another face,
With every question you ask;
Those veils say something,
Masks boast of other,
Which face is to be relied on,
It's difficult to discover.

RECOLLECTIONS IN A WOOF!

These restless nights,
Are mine to battle,
For all those who have been raising arms against me
Are a part of me and my family!
Those dark clouds
Which have crept the clear sky
Are just a mundane level
Of any goofy game!
I ought to step wisely,
In order to escape every error,
Which may befall on my way,
Making the path a terror!
My urge to solve this puzzle is taking me places,
Where I meet kins and some new faces,
None of them could actually comprehend my plight,
Evidently, I am aloof in this flight.

WORDS FROM MUTE

Apparently my clothes can observe and talk,

So my stockings told me how long you have stalked,

That red bra strap peeping through my top,

Noticed in your eyes a hope,

A regular office skirt ,

Hint me that you may flirt,

The scarf covering my chest,

Witnessed your eyes popped at my succulent breast,

Sleeves said they felt uneasy,

When you brushed your hands knowingly,

Each drop which falls on my cheek,

Has sensed your reek,

My thumping heart,

Wishes to slap you hard,

So the next time you have an evil desire,

Beware!

A complaint can get you ensnared.

DEAR HUSBAND

It was all red,
The sky, the moon, and the room,
Seems the night has brought with itself some gloom,
On the bed, there was a white sheet,
Glittering, for it's silky and neat,
There awaits the beast inside,
As if it was the night,
He has been waiting for whole life,
He took me to the bed,
With a grin and a devilish idea in his head,
I was seen as a ripen fruit,
Pressed his palm on my mouth making me mute,
He peeled off my veil,
There was nothing left to conceal,
It took him just a hit,
To get me unfit,
He has got me deflowered,
So that he feel empowered,
And I lie in between that silhouette,
Pondering what made the sheet go velvet,
It was for him that I have come on land,
The notion says, 'bear it, for he is your husband'.

FOOLISH HEART

45

Thoughts loiter with pondering soul,
Will heart fall again in the bleak hole,
Brain clouded by a fake parole,
Befooling it for vague goal,
Foolish love praised in scroll,
Seems to be firing up the petrol,
For how can someone's part be your whole,
Drunken heart deceived by all,
Mountainous desires shrinking in a pothole,
If shattered again, would lose control,
No room will it have for further console.

FATHER

He braced me in his arms,
And I felt heavenly warmth,
He heard my first cry,
Wiped my tears making my cheeks dry,
He taught me to walk,
Stood by my side like a tree of oak,
He held me whenever I fall,
Nurturing in me the lesson to stand tall,
He listened to my babbling words,
Proving that they are not absurd,
He took all my obstacles on him,
Making my path free from grim,
He made me who I am today,
It will be less even if i thank him everyday.

THE CHOICE

Let the fear within you outflow,

This may outshine your glow,

No tear in those eyes should be stopped,

From telling it's story for the time that has been locked,

The clouds of despair will only go,

If you fight something that's holding you low,

You may be standing in the diverging woods,

Choose the road which will lead you to good.

UNLOVED

She cried making her pillow wet,
Setting her heart on fire bed,
Lying all day long on a mat,
Just like that,
No one knows why is she sad,
She has become incoherent,
Faking her smile she lead,
A path so desolate;
She cried making her pillow wet,
Setting her heart on fire bed,
But she doubts if she is set,
To leave all behind and move ahead,
'cause she cannot forget,
Those loved pigment,
To her which are poignant,
Each passing day she lament,
Memorising her love miscreant.

SET FREE

She is the free bird,
Whom he caged,
She wishes to fly high,
But her wings are ragged;
He wings are her will,
Which he already steal;
She's now left with feathers,
Her happiness is long back tattered,
She often chirps to her master,
"set me free it's my weather",
The cruel master does not bother,
Her handful desires he slaughter;
Then one fine night,
Came the knight,
Set her off the clutches tight,
Making her reach the wishful height.

HEAVEN OR HELL

Two places to go,
Heaven or hell;
One will go heaven,
Unless his good deeds sell;
Heaven being a wonderful space,
Consisting mighty well,
Hell in lieu a spot,
Untidy and unwell;
Believed it is, to heaven
Goes a man – angel,
And to hell go all,
Who in life were sinful;
Those satanic acts,
Make them to be thrown in hell,
Provided heaven to those,
With works benevolent and well;
Satan being evil, possesses
The power most devil,
Gods being kind have
All strength angelic;
The life after demise ,
Is not easy, our soul
Has to undergo a process,
Where it will be marked a price;
That very price will determine,
Out of two places to go,
Where it will rest in peace,
Either heaven or hell.

MY PLIGHT

Today they don't stop,
I wish to shout out loud,
I urge to cry my heart out,
I'm clutched by this ache,
I'm a geek for a sake,
I fear to share,
The emotions I hold,
To hurt you I cannot dare,
For my words so bold;
I prefer keeping shut,
I cry, I die in my own hut,
So step back,
Please stay there,
You can never understand,
What it is to be here.

A CONDOLENCE

My heart black and blue,

My mind has no clue,

Like nerves get blocked with achoo,

My movements halt with words few,

Those inedible words I had to chew,

Turning situations to stew,

I chose what has only been left to do,

To my understanding alienating seemed better than to glue,

Ugly, peculiar and clumsy could define me true,

On me these words he often threw,

I try to step into a life new,

Where I may rise from the regiment of jew.

THE PROPOSAL

When I'm afraid,
I'll hold your hand,
When I need some shade,
I'll hold your hand,
When I'm at my lowest,
I'll hold your hand,
When I need someone closest,
I'll hold your hand,
When I'm broken,
I'll hold your hand,
When I need affection,
I'll hold your hand.
I'll hold your hand forever,
Will you too?

SINFUL SATURDAY

It was Saturday night,
And we were delight,
Till we boarded that Bus,
Which proved to be harmful for both of us,
To my wonder,
No one other than two of us was under,
The roof of that four wheeled vehicle,
My heart sank when driver stopped the bus in a desolate
place and my words start to fumble,
We fathers our courage,
And asked driver in rage,
"What's the matter,
Can't you stop at place ant better?"
Suddenly some men break into the bus,
Soon that public conveyance which was the safest turned
out to be most dangerous,
First, they beat my friend till he was almost dead,
Then they looked at me as if I was a meal for them, they
were waiting to be fed,
They took my clothes off,
And my dignity with words of scoff,
I begged for mercy,
Each of them put off his jersey,
One by one they did me wrong,
Limits were crossed when one of them inserted an iron
rod into something that was under my throng,
I cried out loud,

But my voice was inaudible among those dreadful sounds,
After pacifying their thirst,
They threw me on the road as if I'm an iron full of rust.
My soul left my body,
After being lying naked for hours on the road,
When taken to hospital, doctor said to save me there's no
mode.
I pity on humanity and sometimes laugh too,
In name of It, millions of people take part in candle march
when there's nothing left to do.

SELF ESTEEM

My credulity is mine,
If you find it blue,
That's fine!
My actions are carefree,
Not every time to your opinion,
They may agree.
My words keep a check,
Where to put a step,
For they are aware of the deck.
I outshine my own beam,
Perhaps it blinds you,
But I cannot compromise my esteem.